## CREATING A HOME

# CREATIVE IDEAS WITH
# COLOUR

WARD LOCK

# CONTENTS

© Ward Lock Limited 1988
Villiers House, 41-47 Strand, London WC2N 5JE, a Cassell Company
Reprinted 1992, 1993, 1994 (**Twice**)
Based on *Creating a Home*,
First Edition © Eaglemoss Publications Limited, 1986

ISBN 0 7063 6729 4

Printed in Spain by Cayfosa Industria Grafica

# INTRODUCTION

Different from most books about colour scheming, this volume takes fifteen colour groups in turn, and demonstrates the atmosphere and mood each one creates, and how they can be used successfully. Each chapter starts with a comprehensive sample board showing wallpapers, paints, fabrics, carpets and accessories in shades of the colour in question. Then a wealth of colour photographs of room settings makes it easy to understand the infinite variety of effects you can achieve once you know how the different colours work, and how they interact with other colours; and each chapter ends with a page of photographs and drawings showing how to choose and use accent colours.

**Creative Ideas with Colour** starts with the quiet colours which work so well in the smaller home: naturals, beige, neutrals and cream. They show how to use these subtle colours to create settings which are light and spacious, but never dull.

Photographs in the yellow chapter show how its many shades, from light primrose to deep yellow ochre, can be used to stunning effect. The peach and pink sections demonstrate why peach has become one of today's most popular colours, and how pink has come out of the nursery. Green and blue are featured in soft shades of mid-blue and sea-green, to show how these cool colours, teamed with suitable accents, can be used in any room in the house.

If you have large rooms or a taste for the exotic, the chapters on reds and plums, purple, violet and mauve will make your mouth water. Or if you want something completely different, there are schemes using black and white, and sparkling glitter effects, and the possibilities of browns and greys are also explored in this comprehensive book.

**Creative Ideas with Colour** is full of new ways to use colour throughout the home, whether your tastes run to soft neutral colours or bright cheerful ones.

# NATURALLY BEAUTIFUL

'Naturals' in interior design covers an enormous range of colours – from the palest of creams through all shades of beige to browns, greys and tans.

All greys and beiges contain colours that can be found in the earth, stone, rocks and grasses. These natural colours contain plenty of brown shades, though brown is not a colour in its own right but a mixture of reds and yellows. Most greys are a combination of blues and greens, although some of those found in nature often contain an amount of green and yellow as well.

Beige, for example, can either be creamy – which indicates it contains some yellow; pinkish – which indicates red; or slightly olive – indicating a mix of green and yellow.

Several natural colours and materials used together in a room scheme can combine to create their own restful, elegant atmosphere by making use of the natural harmony that exists even between different textures and tones of fabric and other materials such as wood.

On the other hand, naturals added to existing schemes can calm down the brightest of hues or have a unifying effect on a mixture of furnishings and colours. For example, a natural-coloured carpet throughout a brightly-furnished room softens the impact and makes it seem more spacious by not interrupting the eye's flow across the room.

### Natural interest
*Inspiration for a natural-based scheme can come from a shell, moss-covered twig or stone. They're full of unexpected colour.*

▽ **Gentle harmony**
Natural-toned fabrics gently echo the wood chair and lamp and wicker-look pottery jug. The walls have been painted with drag technique to give subtle depth to the basic colour.

## NATURALLY INSPIRED

One way that professional designers study colour is to work directly with samples from nature. Here, for example, a group of stones picked up at random from a beach, are carefully matched to colours from a paint chart, a section of which is shown at the top of the page.

Natural colours combined in this way are muted yet still full of character: they have an in-built harmony.

The corner of the sitting room shown on the right takes the harmonious shades of grey, beige, blue and brown contained in the pebbles to create a peaceful atmosphere.

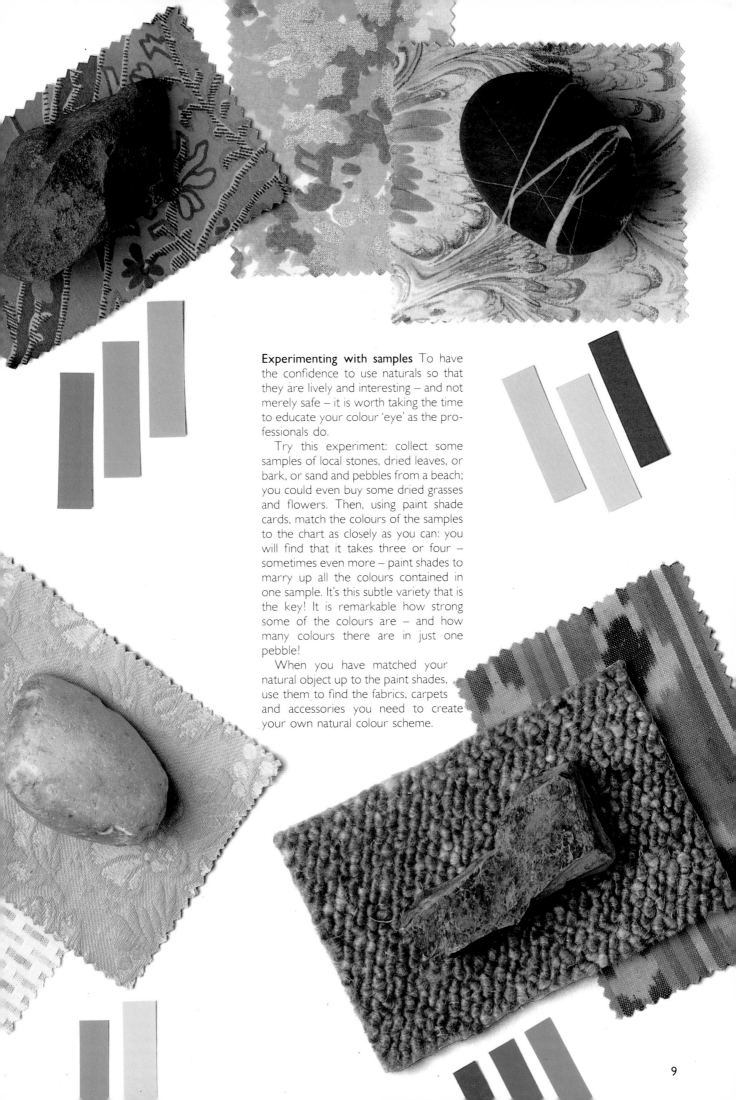

**Experimenting with samples** To have the confidence to use naturals so that they are lively and interesting – and not merely safe – it is worth taking the time to educate your colour 'eye' as the professionals do.

Try this experiment: collect some samples of local stones, dried leaves, or bark, or sand and pebbles from a beach; you could even buy some dried grasses and flowers. Then, using paint shade cards, match the colours of the samples to the chart as closely as you can: you will find that it takes three or four – sometimes even more – paint shades to marry up all the colours contained in one sample. It's this subtle variety that is the key! It is remarkable how strong some of the colours are – and how many colours there are in just one pebble!

When you have matched your natural object up to the paint shades, use them to find the fabrics, carpets and accessories you need to create your own natural colour scheme.

9

## USING NATURALS

Natural room schemes can be warm and welcoming or cool and elegant. Different textures in the same colour range can give quite different effects: for example, soft weaves in upholstery fabrics or shiny chintz cushion material.

In the same way, accent colours can dramatically alter the impression given by a neutral colour scheme: cool blues and greens add to an airy, sophisticated feeling, while the warmer side of the colour wheel – reds, apricots or honey – make a cheerful, friendly room.

To achieve an all-over colour effect, use accents sparingly – three patches are usually enough.

On the other hand, natural-coloured walls and carpeting provide a suitable background for striking colour, which might be in the form of curtains, sofa, or richly-patterned oriental rug.

**Textures and paint finishes** Texture is one way to recreate the subtlety, richness and variety of colours found in natural things. Think of a sleek, silky curtain with a rough linen upholstered sofa; they sit easily with a knobbly wool rug and stained wood table that shows off its grain.

Using paint in colour washes or sponging techniques is also effective, as both depth and subtle variations can be achieved by applying two or three different shades or colours so as to give a translucent or mottled colour. There is also a wide range of wallcoverings available that imitate these techniques and these can be a great boon if you are not too skilled with a paint brush.

△ *Plain and simple*
*Clever combination of several natural colours all contribute to the quiet comfort of this elegant sitting room. The understated charm of simple scrubbed wooden tables and natural sisal flooring offset the sophisticated pearl grey walls and chair covers. Cane furniture covered with plump, feather-filled cushions, and accessories, such as the large urns filled with pampas grasses and the beautifully carved wooden ducks, carry on the natural theme.*

△ **Blue accent**
This cool, sophisticated dining room is enlivened by touches of blue in the tableware and on the walls. The pale beech chairs, with their unbleached fabric seats, stand easily on the natural dhurrie and highly polished wood floor.

▷ **Warm welcome**
Stripped, unvarnished woods with an unbleached linen-look curtain and sisal flooring combine naturally in this hallway. Warm earthy-coloured walls provide a welcoming background that continues the natural colouring.

△ **Dappled shades**
Shades of blue and grey in gently
dappling designs introduce soft colours
and patterns reminiscent of driftwood
or shells found on a seashore. The
natural wool rug remains true to the
overall theme.

▷ **Natural ease**
Stone walls can provide a surprising
amount of colour variation. Here they
form an interesting background for sofa
and curtains made of blue and white
mattress ticking and bright red
embroidered cushions.
   Wicker chairs and table, antique
wood furniture and a wooden curtain
pole are natural accessories.

# BEIGE: BASIC BUT BEAUTIFUL

## Beige is the most versatile of colours and also happens to be one of the easiest to live with.

Beige is usually seen as a neutral, a safe colour to use for the main and most expensive areas of a room. Thus beige is often used as the basis of a room's colour scheme for surfaces and materials which are too expensive to change frequently. These include fitted carpets and sheet flooring, storage units and other major pieces of furniture, tiles and upholstery.

Beige enjoys a reputation for 'going with everything', and it is indeed the most versatile of all decorating colours. But if it is not used with care and imagination, a beige colour scheme can feel dull and drab.

Generally speaking, beige is thought of as a pale brown. It usually contains a hint of another colour such as red, yellow, blue or green. These hints of colour can make the beige appear warm, rich and inviting or, on the other hand, cooler and more reserved.

Obviously, the amount of true colour in a beige is very small. This means that the quantity of black or white that a particular tint of beige contains play a significant role in determining its final shade. For instance, a red-orange beige with a small quantity of white and a slightly larger amount of black will create a sombre colour. One with a lot of white and a fraction of black added will have a distinct apricot tinge. Similarly, a beige which contains a hint of yellow-green can appear almost grey when the black predominates – or it can seem a great deal more sandy-coloured if it is the amount of white which is dominant.

## KNOW YOUR BEIGE

Before you use beige in a colour scheme, it is important to work out what tint of beige will best suit your scheme. In common with other neutrals, beige has chameleon-like properties and is strongly affected by the colours it is seen against.

To see exactly what tint a beige is, place it against samples of the other colours you intend to use. A pinky beige will pick up any reds used in the room and can 'flood' a scheme with red. A beige containing yellow or grey, however, would provide relief and give a crisp edge. With yellow furnishings, consider a greeny-blue beige; with green, a yellow-beige and with blues a beige tinged with pink, apricot, or yellow.

◁ *Beige and white*
*White painted woodwork and mouldings define the important outlines in this mainly beige room. Dark wood provides contrast.*

△ **Beige and blue**
Beige looks restful teamed with natural pine furniture and cool blue furnishing fabrics. The beige background of the fabric calms down the blue and gives a softer, warmer effect than if a white background had been used.

▷ **Sample board**
The curtains and upholstery fabric, together with the wallpaper, used in the room shown above.

◁ **Striking statement**
Persimmon, jade and red above a base of cool beige ceramic tiles, make a striking colour combination that livens up a small bathroom.

## WORKING WITH BEIGE

Beige appears as a 'natural' colour on many surfaces – light woods, wool, linen, raw silk – and so makes an excellent background colour.

While pale colour schemes were popular in the 1960s and 1970s, today's trend is moving towards more highly saturated colours. Try teaming beige with strong shades. Both red-beige and sandy beige look smart with black and white. Beige with smoky grey or navy is another sophisticated combination.

Ethnic designs, too, blend well with beige. Try introducing a dhurrie with beige and a mid-toned colour such as terracotta or petrol blue in the pattern to pep up a mainly beige colour scheme. If the existing colour scheme is based on a pinky beige, then terracotta will liven it up. Similarly, smoky or petrol blue freshen a sandy beige colour scheme.

**Beige and pastels** If you are using beige with pastels choose the clearer, stronger shades such as primrose, sugar pink,

or lilac. Conversely, beige can tone down over-bright colour schemes to produce a quieter atmosphere without making a room seem cold. A warm beige can add a touch of softness to a room where unrelieved white is the dominant colour; it also gives quite a strong contrast effect, even though beige is not considered a strong colour.

**Combining beiges** As with any other colour, different shades and tones of beige can be used together. It is a subtle colour easily affected by the quality of light, so try to match samples away from strong colours and under good natural light.

A pale and dark tone of the same beige can be most effective, while contrasting shades create a harmonious and relaxed atmosphere. Many fabric designs, particularly florals, contain two contrasting beiges – if such a fabric is used for curtains, you can pick out colours from the fabric to add accents for cushions and other small objects. Echo the contrasting beiges on the walls

△ *Gently exotic*
*A beige carpet and walls should be colour matched as accurately as possible as differences in shades of beige over two large areas can be disturbing. Here, the apricot-beige of the walls and carpet are matched to the beiges in the upholstery fabric and blend well with cool greens, warm peachy pinks and soft browns for a lively, exotic look.*

and floors and in any upholstery fabrics the room demands.

**Textures** As with other neutrals, textures are important. An all-beige colour scheme will look more interesting if it involves plenty of contrasting textures. Combine rough, tweedy carpets and loosely-woven linen with smooth, matt leather, shiny satins and silks.

Beige walls and carpets also create a perfect foil for rich mahogany and pine furniture.

◁ **The warmer side of beige**
Indian dhurries offer great inspiration for colour schemes as seen with this dhurrie woven in off-whites, beiges, and pinky terracotta. The terracotta has been echoed in the curtains and door paint.

▽ **Feminine looks**
Beige is a versatile colour that can be interpreted as masculine or feminine. Here, soft pink-painted coving and cushion details accent a light creamy-textured bedspread and the greeny beiges of the room's overall scheme.

## USING ACCENTS WITH BEIGE

In common with other neutrals that may look dull on their own, beige benefits from brightly-coloured accents. Cheerful primary accessories can liven up sober beige schemes.

△ *Harmonious yellow*
*Soft gold harmonizes with, and so emphasizes, the red and yellow tones in warm beiges.*

△ ***Bright blue***
*Towels cool down the warm beige tiles of this bathroom.*

△ ***Sophisticated burgundy***
*Rich wine-red brings out the pinky-brown tones in beige and adds a note of sophistication and warmth.*

# ADVENTURES WITH NEUTRALS

## Infinitely versatile, neutrals are essential to the decorator's palette.

Neutrals play an important part in most decorating schemes providing a useful, unobtrusive background for displaying stronger colours.

In theory the only true neutrals are black, white and pure greys. But for the purposes of decorating, colours which are nearly neutral – whites and greys with a hint of colour (such as off-whites), beiges, greys with a hint of yellow or pink – are termed neutral.

True neutrals can be rather flat and dull and are not much used when decorating. This is especially true in northern Europe where – because of the cool, low light – the warmer greys, mid beiges and pale creams have tended to be more popular.

Neutrals abound in nature. Pebble beaches are exciting symphonies in greys and beige. Ravens' plumage, driftwood, slate and coal are natural vari-ations on a neutral theme. On a more sophisticated level, offices have long enjoyed the practical virtues of neutral decor. Pale greys and white are light and spacious and provide the ideal setting for brightly coloured equipment, while deep grey carpets age well.

Anyone about to decorate a small house or bedsitter would be wise to consider the restful and versatile qualities of using a neutral colour scheme that can be pepped up with bright accent colours. Used with skill, whites, pale greys and beiges can also usefully tone down or bring into focus bright primary colours.

### Versatile neutrals
*These white kitchen units provide a neutral background that goes well with any other colour. A change of blind with a few well-chosen accessories are all that's needed for a new lease of life.*

## USING NEUTRALS WITH COLOUR

Look at most successful colour schemes and you'll find a neutral somewhere. Perhaps white paintwork to emphasize and give a crisp edge to a patterned wallpaper or to act as a link between the paper and flooring. Too much strong colour can be overwhelming and many patterns are on neutral grounds which provide relief from the areas of colour while bringing them into focus.

If you are the kind of person who likes to change things frequently consider a basically neutral scheme with a few strong colour accents such as bright cushions, throwovers, rugs and lampshades.

## A NEUTRAL DECOR

Texture and tonal contrast become all-important to an all-neutral theme; using too many similar greys or beiges can too easily turn into a colour scheme that just looks dull and bland.

Contrasting brilliant white paintwork against black furniture as in very modern styles is one way of overcoming the problem. If you are set on a pale neutral scheme — an all cream or white, say — be sure to provide plenty of textural contrast: look out for nubbly weaves, textured carpets, lace, or shiny glazed cotton. Being light in colour, the textured surfaces will throw strong shadows and provide added interest.

△ *Neutrals as the link*
*Creamy beige sculptured rug and grid pattern walls create a perfect backdrop for this seating arrangement. The two co-ordinating upholstery fabrics also share a neutral, off-white background which allows otherwise busy patterns space to 'breathe'.*

Mid grey walls, flooring and furniture
need colourful relief to avoid looking
dull and cold. Here, cane panels on grey
stained wood chairs appear yellow;
bright flowers and table accessories also
pep up this monochromatic scheme.

▷ **Light and airy**
Cream walls and carpet provide a
spacious, calm backdrop that helps to
emphasize the lines of traditional
dark mahogany furniture. This kind of
very plain, neutral colour scheme often
benefits from a strong focal point: a
boldly-patterned upholstery fabric, or
some dramatic colour in a painting or
flower arrangement.

## KNOW YOUR NEUTRALS

Neutrals need to be chosen with care. The beige which looked just right in the shop may look quite different when placed next to your wallcovering and curtain fabric. If you look closely you will see that most of the different greys and beiges belong to a particular colour group which is either reddish, bluish or yellowish, or a mixture of these. Place a piece of red fabric next to a pinky-beige and it will pick up the red and appear very much warmer and pinker, whereas a greeny-beige will be obviously cooler. If you have a lot of light wood you might find a yellowish beige makes your scheme overwhelmingly yellow and that a bluish beige is a better answer.

△ *Neutrals for toning down*
*Vibrant yellow curtains are a dominant feature of this room. White walls and woodwork with cream upholstery highlight the yellow but tone it down at the same time. Pale grey-blue would have the same calming effect.*

## △ Framing effect
The neutral white walls and a beige and white carpet in this living room have the effect of isolating objects and visually 'framing' them so they stand out more clearly. Fabric patterns and colours are also emphasized and allow the rich reds and complicated pattern variations in the cushions to show up more clearly.

## ▷ Cooler aspects
These provençal-style prints in blues and greens have similar patterns to the ones shown in the picture above and would also work well with a neutral colour scheme giving it a cooler emphasis.

◁ **Points to consider**
First, know your neutral.
Beiges and greys are
available in many different
colour groupings. When it
comes to neutral colours in
carpets it's important to pick
one that complements both
fabrics and wallcoverings. It is
worth experimenting with
several different neutral
carpet samples and noting
which one has a red, yellow
or blue bias. Both fabrics and
wallcoverings could then be
made to feel warmer or
cooler depending on your
carpet choice. For instance
the broken stripes in the
fabric here are in yellowish
and reddish greys while the
square motif in the middle is
a pale bluish grey. If a cool
effect is wanted, choose a
bluish grey carpet; for a
warmer effect try a camel-
colour carpet.

▷ **Neutral choices**
These two fabrics could go
with any of the neutral paint
colours here depending on
the effect wanted. For a
cooler neutral scheme, pick
out pale blue-greys and
green-beiges for walls and
paintwork; for warmer
schemes pinky-beige and
ecru would work well.

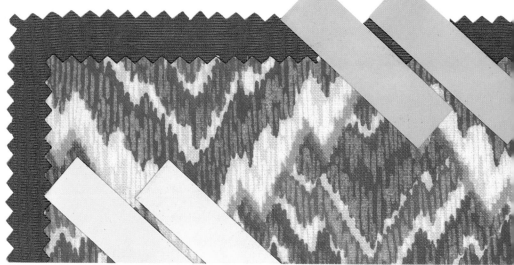

▷ **Playing the neutrals game**
This diagram using paint chip samples shows what kind of
neutral creams, beiges and greys are needed to link the
colours here. Starting with a mid blue paint chip in the
centre, yellow, sage green, caramel and rust chips were
then arranged around. Different shades of grey, cream and
beige were then selected to act as a 'bridge' or linking
device between each pair of strong colours.

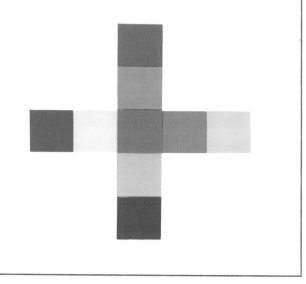

# CREAM – THE KIND COLOUR

Cream is good news for cold climate colour schemes as it creates space and light with a touch of warmth.

As a yellow with white added to it, cream ranges from delicate parchments and ecru through to deeper buttery shades of old ivory and clotted cream. When it comes to faded antique furnishings and old tapestries cream walls are kinder than stark white, and cream also has a softening effect on harshly bright modern furnishings.

Cream was a top colour with famous 18th-century architect, Robert Adam, who knew how cream could enhance rooms lit with diffused English light. By adding gold and white plasterwork he created the perfect backdrop for his rich mahogany furniture.

The Victorians used creamy lace to trim everything – from tablecloths to mantelpieces. After this era, cream suffered a decline and it took the 1920s and 30s to revive it as a major decorating colour. Cunard liners and Hollywood interiors were full of rich creams teamed with blonde bird's eye maple; pale primrose-creams teamed with pastels, white and gold furniture.

Today's all-cream interiors need dramatic handling if they're not to become bland and insipid. Roughly textured cream fabrics, sculptured carpets; sponged and rag-rolled paint effects help. Colour accents to use with cream include soft pinks, blues and black.

△ **Symphony in cream**
Cream has a soft,
filtered, almost romantic
quality that feels eternally
sunny.

▽ **Touches of cream**
Use creamy lace, fringes and
textured, woven and
embroidered fabrics for
definition.

**△ Light and informal**
Cream flatters both light and dark woods and blends particularly well with this plain ash Shaker-style furniture. Painting walls cream rather than white prevents the room looking stark and helps to give an informal, almost country cottage, atmosphere.

**▷ Raspberries and cream**
Romantic horizons are viewed through this creamy lace austrian blind, the pink bows look less strident than they would with white lace. The mahogany vanity unit helps to give a formal, classical air to this delightful bedroom corner. The whole colour scheme would work equally well if soft turquoise was used instead of raspberry.

## WORKING WITH CREAM

Regard cream as a colour in its own right. Choose crisp white woodwork and fabrics to stop cream looking as though it is a white discoloured by age.

Cream is also essentially romantic: think of the rich creamy ivories of antique linens and lace – these were never harsh whites. It's a natural colour, easier to live with than stark white; cream conjures up visions of farmhouse dairies, raw silk, unbleached wool, linen and calico.

In all-cream colour schemes, textured carpets, wallcoverings and furnishing fabrics are important; lace and all kinds of slub weaves, embossed and anaglypta wallcoverings help to add interest. Cream floors reflect light: lay cut pile and sculptured carpets – or creamy tiles in polished marble or textured vinyls.

### △ Blue and cream

*Billowing curtains of creamy voile give a sunny-all-the-year-round feeling. Cream teamed with powder blue woodwork feels warm and luxurious. Modern dhurries use lots of cream. The striking patterns and colours of the one here echo the fabrics and wallpaper to perfection. Crisp white sheets and pillowcases make the cream bedding fabric seem almost pinky-beige.*

△ **Country house cream**
While traditional, the choice of cream gives this room a modern airy feel. It's interesting to imagine how this room would look if typically Victorian wine velvet curtains and upholstery were substituted – most of the light would be lost. Today's cream furnishing fabrics look warm and luxurious and reflect the light; they can also be dry cleaned and pre-treated to repel stains.

◁ **Cream and grey**
Cream is a dramatic backdrop to dark blues and grey. Cream throwovers match the carpet and lighten dark sofas. Even the ceiling mouldings have been painted cream. A splash of dusky pink in the woodcarvings and flowering amaryllis off-set the sombre greys.

# CREAM WITH THREE ACCENTS

Cream has chameleon qualities – it reflects surrounding colours and quietens down harsh tones.

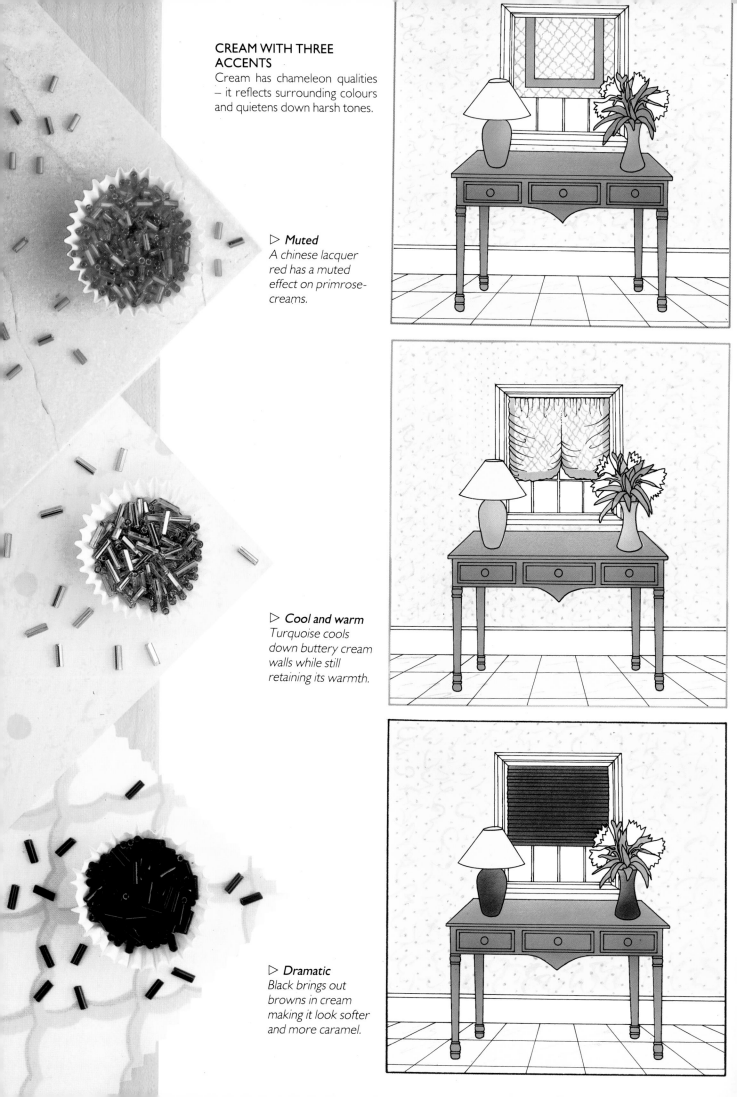

▷ *Muted*
*A chinese lacquer red has a muted effect on primrose-creams.*

▷ *Cool and warm*
*Turquoise cools down buttery cream walls while still retaining its warmth.*

▷ *Dramatic*
*Black brings out browns in cream making it look softer and more caramel.*

# A TOUCH OF YELLOW

Yellow – the colour of sunlight, sand and daffodils – brings warmth and light into your colour schemes.

Yellow in all its many shades is a warm and cheerful colour. Pure yellow is a primary colour, which is very bright and can be hard to handle; but there are many other shades – pale, delicate primrose, lemon, rich buttery tones and deep ochres, for example – which can be soft and mellow, or light and sunny, and are not nearly so daunting to use.

On the colour wheel, pure yellow is equidistant from red and blue – the other two primaries. The tones of yellow, such as lemon yellow, which move towards blue have a sharper, slightly astringent feel to them; the tones closer to red become warmer and warmer, gradually approaching apricot, peach and orange.

## STYLES AND ACCENTS

Yellow suits any style of decoration. For a modern, bright and cheerful look mix pure yellow with other primaries and white; or for a soft and more traditional feel, reminiscent of the pastel shades used in the 18th century, mix primrose yellow with greys, apricot or pale blue.

Yellow makes a very refreshing accent colour, too. The sharpness of lemon adds zest to a neutral colour scheme of greys and white, or beiges, perhaps; a cool mixture of blues and greens can easily be warmed up with a few careful touches of sunny yellow.

## NATURAL MIXTURES

A colour combination found in nature is a good starting point for planning a decorating scheme – cool sky blue and the pastel yellow of the summer sun, for example; or buttercup yellow and grass green, for a more powerful mixture.

Warm tones, such as apricot, orange or pink teamed with yellow, make successful harmonious schemes which are comfortable to live with. The colours in honeysuckle for instance – soft pink and creamy yellow – go together easily.

Like other warm colours, yellow used in wallcoverings makes a room look smaller. A strong daffodil yellow will turn a spacious but stark room into a welcoming space.

### ▷ Strong contrasts
*One way of dealing with strong colours is to put them with other strong colours. Here a daffodil yellow colour scheme is anchored by the dark green carpet. Small touches of dark green – in the plants and on the sofa – and exotic patterns make a striking contrast.*

### ▽ Clean lines
*Two tones of yellow – on the walls and pinstriped upholstery fabric – make a dramatic contrast with accents of black in this very modern living room.*

◁ **Finishing touch**
The small details of a room scheme need as much thought as the larger elements. Here pale yellow coloured kitchen cupboards are given added decoration by painting the moulding inside the panels a more intense tone of yellow.

▽ **Restful tones**
The warm golden yellow walls give this spacious dining room an inviting and restful atmosphere – with such a high ceiling it might have turned out cold and stark. A plain white ceiling and decorated cornice, and a cream carpet balance the rich yellow walls and set off the highly polished antique furniture. The floral fabric of the full-length curtains mixes white with touches of yellow.

▷ **Bright and light**
Pure yellow is a strong and
vibrant colour and needs to
be used carefully. The bold
colour and broad stripes suit
the clean modern lines of this
dining room. Combined with
white in crisp stripes and
plains, it creates a warm
sunny atmosphere without
being overpowering. Notice
how the fireplace has been
picked out by reversing the
stripes.

▽ **Red, yellow and blue**
Yellow works well with the
other primary colours – red
and blue. This small
bedroom, with its sloping
ceiling and walls painted in
the same tone of deep
yellow, has a cosy feel to it.
The yellow provides a strong
background colour for the
blue of the bedcover and the
red of the armchair cover.
The combination of these
three contrasting colours
creates a lively effect.

△ **Pastel tones**
In this elegant living room, a restful atmosphere is created
using pastel tones. A delicate primrose yellow is successfully
mixed with two tones of grey. A variety of patterns – floral
and stripes – are used in wallpaper, border and upholstery
fabrics (samples below).

## USING ACCENTS WITH YELLOW

A variety of visual textures and patterns –
stripes, trellis and marbling – are combined
to create interest in this soft yellow colour
scheme. The addition of accent colours in a
few areas can produce different effects.

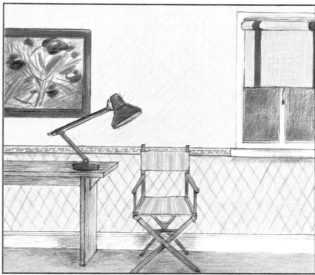

*Accents of leaf green such as the angled work light and the
wallpaper border add cool touches to the scheme.*

*Yellow with purple, which is a mixture of the other two
primary colours, combine well to make a lively contrast.*

*A few charcoal-grey accents add a subtle but sophisticated
touch to this simple colour scheme.*

# ALL ABOUT PEACH

A wide range of tones from fresh
pastels to rich warm hues, make
peach a versatile decorating colour.

Colours go in and out of fashion. In the
early 18th century, soft pastel shades,
such as pink, peach, apricot or pale blue
were popular decorating colours.
Wooden wall panelling was never left in
its natural state, it was often painted in
very delicate pastel shades.

Later, after the dark greens, ochres
and browns popular in Victorian times,
light colours became fashionable again.
Rooms gradually became less cluttered
with furniture, walls were no longer
decorated with collections of pictures in
dark frames and furnishing fabrics and
wallcoverings became lighter. In the first
ten years of this century white was
internationally the most fashionable colour while peach was a particularly
popular choice in the Art Nouveau
interiors of the period, often combined
with a light grey-green.

Peach is also one of today's most
popular decorating colours. It is used on
walls, ceilings and floors. Designs for
furnishing fabrics, wallpapers and floorcoverings combine peach with all sorts
of colours – greens or blues to make
fresh lively mixtures; or pinks, apricots
and yellows for warm harmonious effects.

## SHADES OF PEACH

Peach comes from the warm side of the
colour wheel, and is made up of yellow,
red and white. It is a soft colour with a
pinkish tinge which distinguishes it from
the more orange-yellow shades of
apricot. At its darkest, peach moves
towards terracotta, but add more and
more white to the basic mixture and
you can create a range of the most
delicate pastel tones.

Peach is a very versatile colour. It
works equally well in all sorts of rooms
large or small, traditional or modern.
Add a pale peach to a mixture of subtle
tones such as dusky-pinks or silver-
greens, for a more traditional look; or
bring a warm touch to the cool hard
looks of high-tech colours such as slate-
grey or jade. It brings out the tones of all
kinds of woods, too, from the lightness
of beech or white oak, to the rich dark
tones of antique mahogany or walnut.

## WORKING WITH PEACH

The subtle shades of peach create equally subtle changes in the atmosphere of a room according to the way in which the colour is used.

The blushing middle tones of peach create a warm welcoming atmosphere. It's an ideal tone for a hallway, for instance, where first impressions should be inviting. In a large room a deep peach draws the walls inwards making it feel cosier, but a light tone warms up a small room without making it feel any smaller.

Deep peach contrasted with light colours such as cream emphasizes how sensuous it can look – like peaches and cream. In contrast, a light peach looks fresh and bright combined with other pastel tones. Peach works well with colours it is found with in nature, too – a rich leafy green, or the deep raspberry and brown-gold of the peach stone.

Peach is a very successful accent in a scheme dominated by other colours. Touches of peach in lampshades or cushions, towels or bathmats, are enough to warm up a cool colour scheme of greens and blues.

▽ *Soft option*
*In this modern bedroom, a very pinky shade of peach is successfully mixed with soft olive green and cream. All the furniture is painted in the same tone of peach, with a darker shade used in the curtains and cushion covers.*

△ *Fresh peaches*
*Pink and peach drag painted units with white handles create a pretty fresh atmosphere in this kitchen. Notice how the panels on the window shutters and the wall cupboards are picked out in a paler tone of peach.*

## ▷ Warm and cool

Here, peach, pink and blue make a fresh and delicate mixture. The rosy pink of the floral chintz draws out the pinkish tinge in the peach on the wall behind, making it feel warmer. The peach works well with the pale blue of the lamp and china bowl and the crisp white of the tablecloth. The pink and blue theme is repeated in the floral prints on the wall behind.

## ▽ Traditional elegance

This colour scheme was designed around the painting over the mantelpiece. Peach and a pale grey-blue dominate and are mixed with other neutral tones to create an elegant feel in a traditional room. The soft peach of the walls is picked out in the trellis design of the floor rug, the cover on the sofa, the lampshades and ashtray.

## ▽ Peaches and cream

The colour scheme for this pretty bathroom was inspired by the pinks and peaches found inside the seashells used to make the mirror frame.

The neutral tone of cream used for the bathroom suite makes a good partner for a variety of shades of pink and peach. The walls are painted in two shades of peach above and below the cream dado rail. The deep pink of the drape over the window adds a strong accent to a delicately blended colour scheme.

△ **Peach and grey**
*In this light and airy bedroom the pale shades of peach and grey-blue are a perfect choice to create a restful atmosphere. The fabric of the scatter cushions and tablecloth and the wallpaper border combine peach with the pale grey-blue of the painted cane furniture. The plain blue fabric has been added as a cool accent. The patterns and textures used in the room are shown close up in the samples (left).*

## COOL ALTERNATIVES

Tones of peach work well with a wide range of cool colours, either pastels or strong rich shades. A patterned fabric which mixes peach with a cool colour is a good starting point for planning a colour scheme.

Delicate pale peach used on the wall and floorcoverings provides a warm shell for cooler shades, such as sky blue, or pale jade, used in the furnishings – upholstery and curtains. The result is a well-balanced pastel colour scheme.

In predominantly cool colour schemes touches of peach take the edge off the coolness. A high-tech interior, which is dominated by dark greys and black, and hard smooth surfaces, is softened slightly with accents of a warm deep peach, for instance. Peach can work equally well as a fresh pale accent in a cool pastel scheme.

▷ *Equal tones*
*Peach and a fresh pale green are equally balanced in this traditional bathroom. The minty green of the walls and woodwork is warmed up by the pretty peach design on the paper border, tiles and matching blind. Towels and flannels in matching colours make perfect finishing touches.*

▽ *Chilled peaches*
*Peach works well with the coolness of blue in either modern or traditional rooms. In this modern living room the walls are painted in two tones of peach. The covers on the sofas and the blind combine peach with pale blue in a floral and abstract design to cool down the overall effect.*

## PEACH WITH THREE ACCENTS

The feel of a room can be easily changed with the careful choice of different accent colours. In these three room schemes the same furnishing materials are used, in a range of peach tones. By adding different accent colours in a few small areas – the piping on the sofa, the cushion or the tiebacks for the curtains – quite different effects are created.

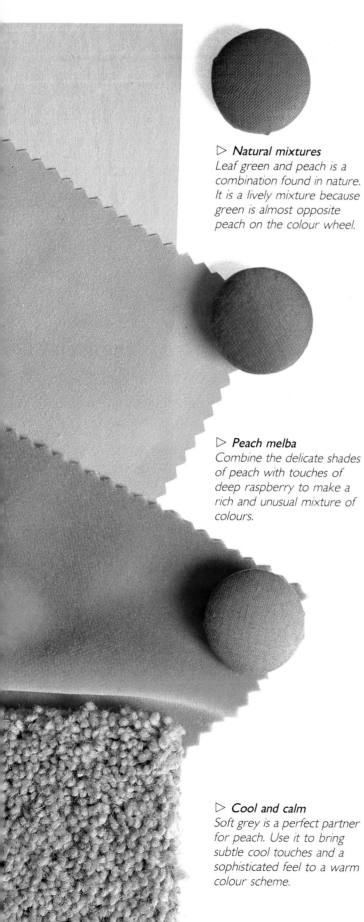

▷ **Natural mixtures**
Leaf green and peach is a combination found in nature. It is a lively mixture because green is almost opposite peach on the colour wheel.

▷ **Peach melba**
Combine the delicate shades of peach with touches of deep raspberry to make a rich and unusual mixture of colours.

▷ **Cool and calm**
Soft grey is a perfect partner for peach. Use it to bring subtle cool touches and a sophisticated feel to a warm colour scheme.

# IN THE PINK

## From softest pastel to the eye-catching bright, pink adds warmth to any scheme.

Pink, being a mixture of red and white with occasionally blue or yellow, comes from the warm side of the colour wheel. Often dismissed as a 'little-girl' colour, pink has hidden qualities. From rosebud to raspberry, through to fuchsia or Schiaparelli's 'shocking pink', it brings life to any colour scheme. A room with a cold aspect feels much warmer if pink is added as an accent or contrast colour. Inspiration can be found everywhere you look in nature – palest pink-tinted clouds against a blue sky or early blossom against leafless branches. Above all, pink sits well with green – whether the new leaf that backs pink-and-white apple blossom, or the greyish tint of the leaves of old-fashioned garden pinks.

Different shades of pink mingle gloriously with a host of other colours in traditional herbaceous borders. This mixture is echoed to perfection in the classic floral designs used for traditional-style room schemes.

In modern urban settings, startling bright pinks serve as emphatic accent colours against severe black-and-white decor, or can soften and warm a monochromatic scheme of greys or beiges.

## PREDOMINANTLY PINK

If you choose pink as the predominant colour in a room scheme, it can be highly successful – but needs careful handling if you want to avoid an ice-cream pink impression. Subtle patterns in wallpapers, borders and fabrics, and a mixture of tones and textures in fabrics and flooring bring variety to one-colour schemes.

Pink in particular offers a wide choice of shades to mix and harmonize. Clear white accentuates the palest pastels while touches of cream soften strong vibrant hues.

◁ *Strong salmon pink*
*Here the walls successfully emphasize the background pinks of curtains and upholstery. Acid green and yellow in the curtains would be more dominant if the walls were pale blue or green.*

▽ *Dream of pink*
*Palest pink walls make a soft backdrop for other, deeper shades – from brownish-pink picture mounts and a sharp pink lampshade to true rose pink in the flower arrangement. White paintwork forms a crisp, clear accent.*

### △ Bathroom for relaxing

Gentle shades of pastel pink and cream impart a truly restful air to this bathroom. The scheme is saved from monotony through lack of tonal variety by the austrian blind which features bold, almost coral, flowers. The green accents of plants echo the leaves in the design, which is picked up in the small pattern on the armchair.

▽ Samples of the three fabrics used in this room scheme.

## ACCENTS TO USE WITH PINK

The very paleness of some pinks makes them the ideal foil for strong accent colours. As can be seen from these three illustrations, even quite small amounts of accent colour can create different effects within the same room scheme.

△ **Modern touch** Using black as the accent brings a bold modern air to traditional-looking furnishings.

△ **Role reversal** Rich tones of naturally cool blue bring warmth and depth to a light pastel pink room scheme.

△ **Natural mix** Pink and green are natural neighbours, and a clear emerald adds life and verve to the delicate pink.

# MID-BLUE –
# A COOL APPROACH

## Use mid-blue to create fresh crisp colour schemes or to add a cool touch to a warm range of tones.

Mid-blue is a colour found in nature – the soft blue of summer skies, spring flowers or a sparkling sea – and some of the tones it works best with are partners in nature, too. Warm beiges with mid-blue conjure up visions of sea and sand; the natural combination of rich leaf-green and mid-blue looks good, despite the old saying that blue and green should never be seen.

Historically, this soft tone of blue was a popular decorating colour – in wallpapers, fabrics, tiles and porcelain. In early Victorian times when light tints such as lavender and pink were being used in bedrooms and living rooms, sober colours such as blue seemed more suitable for libraries and dining rooms, in formal flocks and stripes.

Mid-blue combined with white is a traditional mixture which is reminiscent of old Chinese porcelain, or Delft pottery, painted with pictures of animals and birds.

Nowadays, fabrics and wallpapers combine mid-blue with all sorts of colours to suit many different styles from the traditional looks of formal florals to the abstract designs used in modern interiors.

### HARMONY AND CONTRAST

Mid-blue comes from the cool side of the colour wheel. It is a soft subtle tone between the richness of dark blue and the icy coolness of pale blue. Mixing mid-blue with its neighbours on the colour wheel – sage green, lilac or aquamarine, for instance – creates comfortable and harmonious schemes.

Mid-blue works equally well with delicate neutral shades and with warmer colours, such as reds, pinks and yellows. The colour which contrasts most strongly with mid-blue is orange, which is exactly opposite on the colour wheel. It makes a lively accent in a cool blue colour scheme.

## USING MID-BLUE

This soft tone of blue need not be a cold decorating colour. Teamed with warmer tones to take away any chilly feeling, successful colour schemes can be easily created. It is, however, a colour best suited to light rooms; in sunless rooms mid-blue could be oppressive.

The striking combination of mid-blue and white makes an impact when used in a variety of patterns, such as stripes, bold florals, or abstract designs. You can mix and match all sorts of patterns and still be successful by using this, simple combination of colours.

Mid-blue makes a good accent colour, either as an harmonious or contrast accent. In an all-white bathroom, for instance, touches of mid-blue make a sharp contrast and create a crisp and fresh look. It also has a subtle cooling effect in an harmonious scheme of warm colours, such as pinks and peaches, or yellow and beige.

▷ *Subtle shades*
*Mid-blue, pale grey and touches of pink make an harmonious colour scheme in this light living room. The rag-rolled walls bring some visual texture into a room scheme with smooth finishes. The variety of pink tones in the cushions, lamp and curtain fabric act like accents.*

△ *Natural partners*
*A soft tone of mid-blue suits the clean, unfussy lines of this modern but relaxed living room. It goes well with the soft neutral shades of the wood floor, the wickerwork basket and the muslin drape over the window, adding a cool tone to the warm shades of beige. The rug combines all these tones in its simple design.*

△ *Flowery corner*
A traditional-looking floral design is perfect for
this corner window seat with leaded windows
and a garden view. A vivid tone of mid-blue is
teamed with rich shades of pink, green and beige
in three different fabrics. The same tone of mid-
blue is used for the simple rosebud sprig design
on the wallpaper. The variety of patterns are
held together because the same range of colours
is used in each of them.

◁ *Cool blues*
Mid-blue and light blue mixed with
white and gleaming chrome accessories
give this traditional bathroom a crisp
fresh feel. Notice how the moulding on
the panels around the bath and the
picture rail are picked out in pale grey.

▷ *Warm and sunny*
A simple mixture of sunny yellow and
mid-blue create a warm restful feel in
this elegant bedroom. The mid-blue of
the mini-print designs on the patchwork
quilt is picked out in the plain stripes in
the curtain fabric and the carefully
shaped pelmets.

△ **Mostly mid-blue**
*Subtle patterns in wallcoverings and fabrics are useful for bringing a variety of textures to colour schemes which are dominated by a single colour and which tend to look flat and boring. In this mid-blue room, several textures have been added in the wallpaper and its border, the upholstery fabric and the trellis-patterned carpet. The fabric for the curtains combines the beige of the carpet with mid-blue in a simple floral design. Samples of the wallpaper and fabrics used in this room are shown left.*

◁ **Blue and white**
A fresh shade of blue and brilliant white is a traditional combination which is always successful in fabrics and wallcoverings. This collection of cushions with two formal but contrasting patterns – stripes and a large paisley design – work well together using the same two basic colours.

▽ **Mixing patterns**
Mid-blue is the perfect choice for this comfortable modern living room. Simple floral and leaf designs which combine a subtle range of colours – dusky pink, soft jade green, for instance – with mid-blue, are mixed in fabrics and wallcoverings creating a cool temperate colour scheme.

## USING ACCENTS WITH MID-BLUE

Mid-blue is a tone which works equally well in all sorts of colour schemes. Combine it with soft pinks and greens for a more traditional look, or with primary colours in a modern scheme. In this modern dining room the black lacquered wood furniture is mixed with mid-blue and a variety of accents to create different effects.

△ *A few touches of shocking pink instantly add life to a simple mid-blue and white colour scheme.*

△ *Touches of yellow in a few areas are enough to bring the warmth of sunshine to a cool blue scheme.*

△ *Shades of mid-blue combined with a rich leaf green is an harmonious mixture found in nature.*

# RESTFUL SEA-GREEN

## Green – especially blue-green – is the most restful on the eye of all the colours in the colour wheel.

Green is situated on the colour wheel between the two primary colours, yellow and blue, and can vary in colour from a very yellowish shade, through astringent lime green, lettuce and apple greens, to sage, peppermint and all the shades of the sea. Opposite it lie the hot oranges, pinks and reds that work so effectively as contrast colours.

Here the blue-green end of the spectrum is focused on, where the shades are softer, cooler and easier to handle in a colour scheme than the harder and more abrasive yellow-greens. This softness of tone means that the paler shades of blue-green can be used in some considerable quantity in a room scheme without becoming overwhelming in any way.

Although green is the colour most widely found in nature, it is surprisingly difficult to extract a natural dye. Dyes from nature tend to give rather pale, often muted shades. These are especial-ly attractive when combined with other soft colours, as shown by work of the 19th century craftsman-artist William Morris whose designs are still popular.

### STYLES AND ACCENTS

The soft blue-greens are ideally suited for cool, sophisticated colour schemes in smart town houses; and they create just the right atmosphere for shady rooms in hot climates. Deep sea-green can make a superb accent colour when used with pastels such as primrose yellow or pink.

Alternatively, pastel blue-green shades can form a harmonious background for many other colours: pinks – either pastel or a bright fuchsia – or yellows, while strong deep blues, such as cornflower, and reds, such as crimson, all make good accents.

Because they are so easy on the eye, pale duck-egg tints and other pastel hues make superb backdrops for naturals.

**△ Fresh and clean**
This light aquamarine colour
is one you can use in quantity
without it becoming
overwhelming. Here it is
used in two tones, with
touches of white for
freshness, coral-coloured
shell stencils for warmth, and
bright cornflower blue (in a
bottle) for a surprising
accent.

**▷ Colour partners**
Here the coral and turquoise
chairs and straw-coloured
mat all make happy partners
with the blue-green walls.
Daylight makes a subtle blue-
green seem bluer, while
electric tungsten light makes
it seem greener: something
to consider when devising a
room scheme.

◁ **Deeper blue-greens**
Rich, deep blue-greens look good in conjunction with clear blue as well as apricot and shades of natural wood or brass. The glowing colours in this patterned chintz could easily dominate a colour scheme. However, a trellis-design wallpaper in pale sea-green and cream results in a pleasing and interesting harmony of patterns and colours.

▽ **A foil for wood**
Duck-egg colour walls make a superb background for every sort of wood and natural leather. They cool the warmth of the wood and, because the colour provides a complete contrast, enhance the sculptural outlines of furniture. Note how the cushions on the leather sofa pick up the blue-green theme in different textures and shades.

### △ Traditionally pretty
Many plants with blue-green leaves, such as rosemary, have mauvish flowers. For a gentle, pretty scheme these colours – from the softest lilac, through warm, grapey blues, to pink – always combine successfully. The deep sea-green trim on the curtain valance provides a note of emphasis.
◁ You can pick out the colours more clearly in these samples.

### ▷ Coolly modern
Modern lines and blond wood are softened by using blue-greens all over the walls and stained floorboards. Note how ivory details – in lights, phone and flowers – look softer than white.

△ **Richly sophisticated**
*Crimson red and black combined with rich blue-green produce a dramatic effect. By introducing beige in the sofa stripe, the designer prevents the scheme from becoming too sombre. Black painted furniture would look well in this setting too.*

## BRIGHT IDEA

**Stencils** in coral, cranberry or woody browns look good on aquamarine-painted surfaces. Incorporating a darker greeny-blue for stencilled foliage links the design to its background.

## USING ACCENTS WITH BLUE-GREEN

Blue-green fits in with any style of decoration, whether modern or traditional, and makes a splendid foil for a wide range of accent colours, such as fuchsia or lilac, peach, coral or terracotta, and many shades of blue – such as cornflower or dark Oxford. In pastel tones it is especially suited to late 18th century and early 19th century styles, being reminiscent of the shades so popular for walls of the period. It also makes a soothing background for modern fabrics featuring strong colours.

△ **Strong accents**
Lilac picture frames, scatter cushions and tieback trim pick up one of the secondary colours in the curtains and contrast well with the marbled wallpaper and upholstery fabric.

△ **Dark and subtle**
With the same plain green carpet, self-patterned sofa and curtains quite a different mood is achieved using a more subtle deep red for the frames, lampshade and tieback trim.

# THE RICHER SIDE OF RED

## Reds and plums are very rich colours: used in the right way they can feel warm and luxurious all the year round.

True red is the strongest, most dominating of all the colours. It is a warm, powerful, advancing colour which, when used in any quantity, can draw in surroundings and make them feel claustrophobic. Used sparingly, red can make objects stand out and become focal points. Even functional objects such as pipework can be transformed into a decorative feature with a coat of glossy red. In the neutral-minded 1980s the orangey-reds have been played down in favour of the cooler, less insistent blue-reds. Combined with the cooler properties of blue, red is calmed down so that it becomes less eyecatching, varying from raspberry through the burgundies to deepest plum.

The softer, rich reds work particularly well in dining rooms that are mainly used in the evening for formal meals. Plum and raspberry are also wonderful

welcoming colours for large hallways and landings, making these areas feel warmer and smaller because they seem to draw the walls closer together. In the same way, a chair upholstered in brilliant cherry red looks bigger and more important than one with deep blue upholstery.

Plums combine well with bright pinks, pale turquoise blues and minty greens. The darker plum shades are also practical colours that do not show the dirt easily. In hallways and landings, some of the small, all-over carpet designs with red backgrounds are a practical consideration. Sponging or rag-rolling walls with plummy reds gives a much needed warmth and softness that can benefit a room with a cold aspect. Contrast these reds with lots of crisp white-painted woodwork and a light creamy-beige floorcovering.

▷ **Pretty with pine**
Pink, blue and beige are a
winning combination with
plum. The same colours have
also been picked out in the
cushions, chair seat and co-
ordinating wallpapers. A
beige carpet and mellow
pine furniture provide a
neutral background for the
busy wallpaper pattern.

▽ **Plum and white**
The use of white sets off the
darker shades of plum and
suits this Victorian bedroom
to perfection. The
patchwork quilt also cleverly
echoes the plum and white
colour theme. A picture rail
and a built-in wardrobe all
painted plum are attractive
features to emphasize.

◁ *Border emphasis*
*A simple red chequered border echoes the pattern in the rug and teams well with bluish-grey painted window mouldings. Touches of red in the flowers and accessories give an instant splash of colour to this predominately neutral cream and grey scheme.*

▽ *Warm and inviting*
*Red is an advancing colour that makes rooms look smaller and works well in areas where one doesn't spend much time. Red also absorbs light, so using a gloss paint for the brilliant red panelling helps reflect any available light.*

## WORKING WITH REDS AND PLUMS

A deep red Persian or Indian carpet is a good base from which to build a colour scheme. These carpets usually contain several muted reds, including plum shades and often one that is· closer to orangey-red.

Try matching these carpet colours to the reds on paint shade cards – the paint samples can then be used to match up other reds in furnishing fabrics and wallpapers.

Shelving, an old table, or a trunk will look very handsome painted in a deep plum eggshell finish – this is easier on the eye than brilliant gloss paint.

A stencilled frieze in a brighter, more orangey-vermilion red on a plum-coloured background makes the plum appear browner and more muted. A pattern in a deep yellow also looks sophisticated. Other good combinations to put with the darker reds and plums are black-stained wood, natural pine or light oak furniture.

Natural wood floors and beige carpets also make a good foil for red walls. But avoid the use of too many boldly-patterned, contrasting red and white fabrics in any one room as these can be overpowering. A geometric mini print in dark red on a beige background is much easier to live with.

▷ **Crisp and modern**
*A smart black and white geometric upholstery fabric sets off these softly sponged red walls and bookshelves to perfection. Striped curtain fabric containing the three colours helps link seating and wall colours together and creates a comfortable and modern reading corner.*

▽ **Framing with red**
*In this room the furnishing is fairly simple; interest is provided by the wallpaper and woodwork. One of the reds from this busy floral wallpaper has been chosen for the window frame and skirting to create a restful break for the eye while at the same time acting as a frame for the design.*

## LIGHTING

Because all reds absorb a lot of light, rooms with predominately red colour schemes need special care when it comes to lighting.

When buying red fabrics it is a good idea to take samples to view under the lighting conditions at home. Reds in fluorescent light can turn uncomfortably blue.

Avoid using translucent red silk lampshades as this not only reduces the amount of light but gives a theatrical pinkish glow which affects other colours in the room. For instance, blues will take on a mauve cast; yellows can turn orange and greens turn brown. If you do choose red lampshades, make sure they are lined in white, or pick cream colour shades which give a more neutral light.

**Pepping up last year's scheme** If you are tired of pastel and neutral schemes, try using reds in ethnic patterned fabrics such as ikat weaves, paisleys, batik prints and kelim rugs.

A beige carpet with sofa and chairs in a pastel floral print and plain beige curtains could be changed dramatically by replacing the upholstery and curtains with a daring ethnic print of plummy reds and adding an oriental rug.

Try and match ceramics and cushion fabrics to the reds in oriental rugs and the upholstery. Spray-painting wicker baskets a deep glossy red gives a bright, festive look.

△ **Exotic contrast**
Red makes objects look larger and more important in a room scheme. The red in the military chests here also brings out the red in the richly patterned curtains behind and prevents them looking too heavy.

▽ **Sample board**
Traditional patterned fabrics with red backgrounds look warm and inviting and combine well with small, geometric mini prints that are very close in tone.

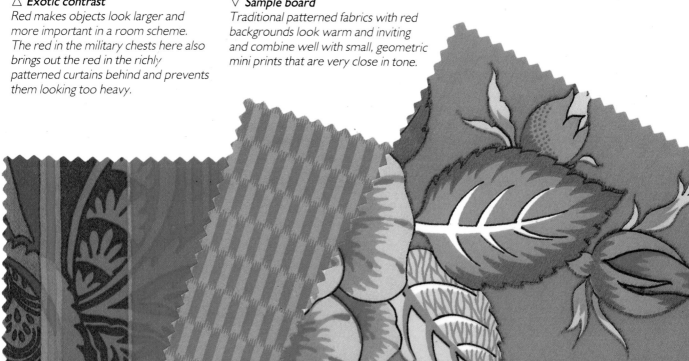

## USING RED AS AN ACCENT COLOUR

As red is such a strong predominating colour over large areas, it is often used as an accent colour to liven up quiet, cool, understated colour schemes.

Red paintwork and accessories – especially in a kitchen – can be replaced after a year or so if you find them overpowering. Try a cooler plum-red for a different effect.

Reds are especially good mixed with sombre neutrals, or the paler blues and greens.

▷ **Red with grey and black**
*Neutral schemes using greys and black can benefit enormously from touches of brilliant colour seen in this red gloss painted window frame, red kitchen sink and accessories.*

△ **Cheering up the blues**
*Cool, receding pastels and mid-blues are brightened up considerably here with cheerful red accents.*

△ **Pepping up the mints**
*Greens lie in direct contrast to reds on the colour wheel; pastel and mint greens look livelier accented with red.*

# SHADES OF PURPLE, VIOLET AND MAUVE

Choose rich purple for drama,
or gentler lilac and lavender
for a more peaceful environment.

Purple has long been associated with royalty: a brilliant purple dye made from a special Mediterranean shellfish was reserved for the Tyrian purple cloaks of Roman emperors because it was both costly and difficult to obtain. As well as the opulence of imperial purple, though, this group of colours includes rich mauve, deep violet and the muted shades of lilac and 'old lady' lavender.

As decorating colours, purple and violet have been out of favour since the psychedelic 1960s when they were seen everywhere from mini-skirts to front doors. Similarly, shades of lilac and mauve have been so little used in interiors over the past decade or so that they could almost be termed 'the forgotten colours'. Now that they are once again becoming more fashionable, we must re-learn how to use them.

Purple, violet and mauve all come from the blue-red part of the colour wheel. Purple contains roughly equal quantities of blue and red and more

black than lilac. Mauve, though, contains slightly more red than blue while violet, on the other hand, has a touch more blue than red.

The richness of deep purple, mauve and violet makes them difficult colours on which to base a colour scheme – just as a brilliant yellow or red room is hard to live with on a day-to-day basis, so is one decorated mainly in purple. Handled well, though, a room with plenty of purple can be effective, especially when offset by a bluish grey.

In contrast, the paler shades of lilac and lavender are much easier to live with – and easier to handle. They are surprisingly flattering colours for bedrooms – daylight shining on lilac walls or through curtain fabrics has a reddish cast that gives a healthy pink glow to the pastiest of complexions! And in other rooms, too, lilacs can form the basis of an eye-catching colour scheme. Queen Victoria favoured pale lavender walls for her bedroom at the Royal Pavilion at Brighton; she teamed this with black papier-mâché furniture inlaid with mother-of-pearl.

## WORKING WITH PURPLES

Brilliant purple and violet are such strong colours that, used in quantity, the effect can be dramatic, not to say overpowering! On the whole, purple walls are most effective in short-stay areas such as halls and cloakrooms where their impact will neither overwhelm the room's occupants nor prevent peaceful relaxation. Strong violet can also be used to great effect in a dining room to create the right environment for formal dinner parties.

In the long run, a bright purple or mauve carpet is not easy to live with either; a pale grey-mauve or light heather would be attractive at floor level and blend well with both pale and dark wood furniture.

If you do base a room scheme on purple, use it with conviction. Team it with other rich colours such as walnut brown, fuchsia red or emerald green – or even gold – to bring out the warmth and drama of the colour scheme. To tone down the overall effect, use fairly neutral accent colours – pale straw, smoky greys, or black for instance.

Tones of mauve, lilac and purple make gentle backdrops for any room when used with a special paint effect such as dragging or sponging which breaks up the solid colour. Team with pinky beige, warm blue or apple green.

### △ Study in purple
Purple walls provide a splendidly dramatic foil for the rich colours of this elaborate collection of antiques and bric-a-brac. The opulent yet plain background intensifies the richness of the gilded picture frame and ornaments, and brings out the deep grain in the walnut chest of drawers. The result is far richer than could be achieved with a pale grey or beige background.

### ◁ Linking with purple
Elsewhere in the same room, the striking walls are balanced by equally strong pinks, reds and blues while the plain treatment of the walls offsets and brings together the busy patterns of the bedcovering and oriental carpet. Large hinged mirrors behind the bed and the warm bamboo and walnut furniture add to the overall drama and richness.

▷ **A symphony of colours**
Almost every shade of
purple and lilac combine
easily in this collection of
hand-painted silk cushions.
Drawing their inspiration
from nature, the stylized
flower motifs demonstrate
the variety of colours which
can sit happily together.

▽ **Cool and modern**
Muted mauve walls and a
mottled grey carpet provide
a quiet backdrop to a sofa
upholstered in a busy black-
and-white design. The
potentially sombre effect of
the dark-toned wall is
tempered by strong lighting
and the clear white lines of
the fire surround.

△ **Formal yet warm**
*Shades of purple ranging from palest lilac to deep violet and rich blue combine to create a rich pattern in the furnishing fabric shown in detail on the left.*

*The strong, somewhat dark pattern is lifted and counterbalanced by plain walls and carpeting in warm beiges and soft subdued lighting. The result is a room which is simultaneously formal and inviting.*

◁ *Sophisticated pastels*
A pale mauve sofa adds gentle warmth and colour to a cool and sophisticated living space dominated by white and the palest of sky blues. Pink flowers and the fronds of an exotic palm provide just enough life and colour to prevent this scheme from looking too cold.

▽ **Trimmed with white**
A white background gives light relief to the regular arrangement of sprigs of violets on the wallpaper and curtains. A plain white-painted dado and a narrow green edging stripe give a crisp edge.

## USING ACCENTS WITH LILAC

Shades of purple vary from pale lavender to deep violet, so choose your accents according to the background's tonal value. Warm up pale pastels with rich contrasts or deeper-toned accents, or keep the feeling cool with colours just a shade or two darker. Enhance the feeling of opulence by teaming deep purple or violet with equally strong coral or gold, tone down the atmosphere with calming blue-greys or heathers, or achieve the perfect balance by using accents of equal strength.

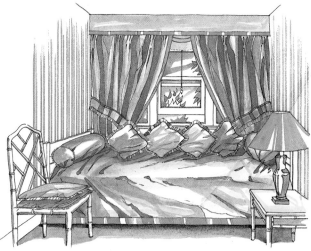

△ **Enliven deep lilac** with accents in warm coral to create an atmosphere that is both rich and welcoming.

△ **Leaf green and lilac** Reminiscent of lilac trees in flower, this combination is inspired by nature.

△ **Charcoal grey accents** neaten the outlines of the gentle drapes of the bedspread and curtains.

# EARTHY TONES OF BROWN

### A room decorated in shades of brown can be warm and comfortable and still look stylishly modern.

In recent years, the earthy shades of brown have been neglected as decorating colours. Labelled dull and boring, browns have tended to take a back seat in favour of more passingly fashionable colours. A close look at the enormous range of browns to be seen in autumn and winter reveals many exciting colour combinations that can be used to introduce a warm, comfortable and muted note.

At its darkest, brown can seem virtually black; at its lightest, it merges imperceptibly into dark beige. In between lies a whole spectrum of shades, from reddish chestnut to dark chocolate, light walnut, and the earthiness of cork.

Brown particularly lends itself to decorating schemes with a rugged, country appeal. Combine brown-based wallcoverings with simple wooden furniture, rush matting on the floor, and natural fabrics such as tweeds, hessian and linen.

Browns can also create sophisticated room schemes. Using closely-related tones combined with rich patterns and fabrics, gleaming mahogany and smooth leather can add up to a very contemporary feeling of richness and depth.

However, if you're aiming for a warm and enclosed feel, beware that the result isn't also too sombre. One way to ensure it isn't, is to use pale accents – a duck egg blue or cream, perhaps – to add life and sparkle to the scheme. Alternatively, go to the other end of the tonal scale – glossy black accents will both gleam and lighten the brown by sophisticated contrast.

## △ Shades of autumn

Thick curtains in a gingery colour with a soft sheen add a touch of softness and warmth to a subtly-patterned wallpaper. An eiderdown with a muted paisley motif and dark wooden bedside furniture complete the brown theme, while touches of cream and white add light and contrast.

## ▷ A touch of brown

When combined with plenty of pale shades, dark brown can appear warm and inviting. In this well-lit bathroom, plenty of dark wood in the door and mirror frames, venetian blind and a highly-polished occasional table, combined with a brown-and-white tiled floor, appears rich and glowing against creamy walls and panelling.

◁ *Warm and welcoming*
An all-brown colour scheme which mixes different shades and textures is particularly easy on the eye, provided there is plenty of light relief. In this entrance hall, the furniture, banister rail and parquet flooring made from a rich, dark variety of woods are set against a delicately-patterned wallpaper which combines a dark and a lighter brown, and stripped pine doors. Brilliant white paintwork adds crispness and definition to the room.

▽ *Gothic inspiration*
The abundance of dark browns in this study corner, together with the subdued lighting, could create a slightly oppressive atmosphere. To combat such a possibility, the designers of this room have introduced gilded picture frames, and furnishing fabrics which include rich chestnut browns and beiges. The black background of the curtain fabric by contrast makes the browns appear lighter and brighter.

## WORKING WITH BROWNS

If you are considering a change from a paler colour scheme to one based on brown, the key issue is lighting. Dark colours quite literally soak up available light. Don't wait until the room is decorated before increasing the lighting – anticipate the need and plan for it. Remember that textures also affect levels of light: glossy surfaces reflect light back into the room while matt or tweedy surfaces absorb it.

To create the basis of a subtle, rich tapestry of colours in a living room, combine several tones of brown or closely-related colours. You'll get inspiration from paisley designs. Alternatively, a fairly dark brown like chestnut below the dado rail and a caramel tone above, can be teamed with a mottled or speckled carpet in dark browns and rusty shades. Introduce slightly shiny finishes such as leather, raw slubbed silk, chrome and brass to add a touch of opulence. Use dark, rich accents for drama or paler shades for a lighter feel.

For a brown bedroom scheme, a patterned wallpaper combining light and darker tones of brown is a good basis. Sponged or rag-rolled walls help to create a hazy feel reminiscent of autumn woodland.

Although wooden fitted kitchens are popular, banks of dark brown kitchen units can feel oppressive – pale, fresh colours such as aquamarine, duck egg blue, or cream on splashbacks, work surfaces and floors as well as in accessories, will all add light relief.

◁ **Brown co-ordination**
Brown-based decorating schemes need not necessarily be traditional in character. In this hall, a mixture of co-ordinating wallpapers, furnishing fabrics and carpeting with earthy tones of deep coral and reddish-brown in common create a modern, sophisticated feeling. The dark brown console table sets off the paler browns around it.

▽ **Sample board**
Samples of the fabrics and wallpapers used in the hall shown above.

△ **Crisply modern**
Spicy cinnamon brown provides an
excellent foil for stark black and white
furniture, woodwork and accessories.
The orange and red tones in the
flowers, fruit and prints emphasize the
warmth of the cinnamon walls and crisp
chequerboard flooring.

▷ **Versatile brown**
Linked by a common colour theme,
different patterns can look good
together: here various brown-based
patterns have been used on the floor,
for the curtains and blinds, and the
upholstered chair and footstool.
Touches of a light blue-green break up
the brown and stop it becoming
overwhelming; the white lifts the
scheme, adding light and freshness.

△ **Pale pink accents** *soften this predominantly brown kitchen.*

## ACCENTS TO USE WITH BROWNS

To 'lift' the atmosphere, team browns with white, pale creams and beiges, or flashes of stronger contrasting colours such as red or purple, royal blue or green.

To achieve a more opulent decorating scheme, use rich colours and strong patterns for accents. Deep azure blue or a raspberry red, and intricate paisleys or elaborate floral patterns, all work well. Grey and black can also bring drama and sophistication to a room where brown dominates.

△ **Royal blue accents** *always look good with natural wood.*

△ **Touches of red** *add vigour to plain brown kitchen units.*

△ **Blue-green accessories** *lighten areas of solid brown.*

# ALL THAT GLITTERS

Metallic finishes can create rooms
with a touch of Hollywood glamour
or a subtler effect with
the merest hint of glitter.

Over the centuries, gold and silver have signified wealth and opulence: ancient Egyptian Pharaohs sat on golden thrones, Aztec kings drank from gold goblets; oriental potentates, on the other hand, preferred gold and silver incorporated into fabrics and ceramics.

Nearer our own time, 18th-century Europeans favoured gilded furniture and silver tableware. Gilding methods reached sophisticated heights and previously dark and heavy furniture was given a new lightness. Opulent brocades woven with gold and silver threads were used for elaborate curtains as well as upholstery – and the interiors of stately homes positively glistened.

The Victorians were keen on gleaming accessories. Polished brass and copper coal scuttles took pride of place at the hearthside;

ornately gilded urns also adorned the mantelpiece.

It wasn't until the 1920s that actual metals as well as metallic finishes came into their own. Polished chrome tubing, the ideal material for a style which stressed the importance of technology, was used to create streamlined seating and table frames.

In the 1980s, the hard, reflective surfaces of metals such as steel and aluminium typify the high-tech look.

Metallic effects can be used very effectively to create any one of a range of styles – from glittering Hollywood glamour to the metals preferred by followers of high-tech style. You can choose highly reflective wallcoverings in mirror-shiny foils or furnishing fabrics with a subtle sheen, mirror tiles in bronze and copper effects or ceramic wall tiles with a hint of glitter in the pattern, even stardust-spangled vinyl floorings.

## △ Formal grandeur

Shades of royal red and gold create an atmosphere of opulence and grandeur in this period dining room. Gently reflective surfaces are found throughout the room – light bounces off the rich wood panelling, the highly-polished dining table and the sparkling crystal and silverware, as well as the gold-printed fabric and wallpaper. A small yet intricate gilt table reinforces the opulent theme. Such a room requires strong but diffused lighting to avoid both glare and too dark an atmosphere.

## ◁ Simply sophisticated

A basically neutral colour scheme provides the perfect backdrop to the understated elegance of this hallway. In the total absence of any pattern, the gilt frame and brass lampshades draw the eye to a luxurious flower arrangement centrally and symmetrically positioned in front of the mirror and between the table lamps.

▷ *Variations on a theme*
*The tall windows in this room are elaborately draped with two fabrics where gold designs have been printed on to dyed cotton. The rich colouring of the oriental carpet and the gilded frame of the chaise longue are echoed by the colours of the curtain fabrics.*

## GLITTER AND GLAMOUR

Metallics demand careful handling: an excess of shiny surfaces in a room can create a restless effect more suited to a discothèque than a home. Highly reflective finishes in wallcoverings, fabrics, paintwork and furniture need to be used fairly sparingly if they are going to add drama and brighten dark surroundings without becoming garish or simply blinding!

In a small or dark room, metallic wallpaper can dramatically increase the feeling of space and light. Fabrics and co-ordinating wallpapers in jewel-rich rubies, sapphires and emerald greens combined with silver or gold can add a festive feeling to a formal dining room and provide a flamboyant backdrop for sparkling china and glassware.

In sunny rooms it's often best to avoid shiny wallpapers which could cause glare, although a textured metallic paper in, say, a muted mint green or pearly blue could add an extra touch of brightness.

Traditionally, costly brocades were woven with gold and silver thread. Nowadays, though, brocades can be woven with gold or silver-dyed silk thread or really shiny lurex. Cottons with gold or silvery overprinted designs make a cheaper alternative for curtains and upholstery.

Mirror tiles or glazed ceramic wall tiles with a shiny gold or silver design can turn the most ordinary of bathrooms into one worthy of a Hollywood star. Used more sparingly (perhaps dotted among ordinary tiles) the result will be less opulent, but perhaps easier to face first thing in the morning!

Metals and glossy enamelled surfaces need contrast and balance if the atmosphere is not to become glaring and harsh. To achieve a richly opulent look, team them with deep carpets and squashy leather sofas. For a more understated effect, combine metals with neutral colours and furniture with strong, simple shapes.

Some shiny foil wallcoverings can create an illusion of light and space similar to that of a mirror. Use them to compensate for the lack of natural light in poky internal bathrooms and hallways. A low ceiling covered in a silvery paper will appear higher, lighter and brighter.

▽ *Sample board*
*The fabrics used in the room above are each shown here in two colourways.*

△ **A modern feel**
The modern metal shelving and glass table in this room are offset by a colour scheme composed almost entirely of shades of grey and off-white. The shiny blinds and sofas upholstered in a velvety fabric with a slight surface sheen complete the eminently cool and restrained atmosphere.

◁ **Light and airy**
Room dividers do not have to be solid panels. Here, a curtain of metallic discs partitions off a dining area, giving a degree of privacy without interrupting the overall feeling of space and lightness.

The metallic theme is carried through to the chrome chairs and highly reflective table, which in turn mirrors the zigzag pattern of the window blind.

## WATCHPOINTS

Bear the following points in mind if you plan to use shiny wallcoverings or fabrics in your home.

**Walls** must be completely smooth since shiny wallcoverings – especially in large patterns or plain colours – ruthlessly highlight imperfections. Small all-over patterns can be a better choice since they tend to show faults less.

**Lighting** very shiny mirror foils needs careful planning to avoid dazzling people. Fitting dimmer switches to existing lighting reduces uncomfortable reflected glare; soft uplighters and directional downlighters that point the light source away from the reflecting surface are also a good idea.

**Accessories** If a metallic wallcovering is part of a room scheme, it's often best to choose accessories such as door furniture, kitchen and bathroom taps, and light fittings in metal finishes. But make sure they match: for instance, chrome taps may look out of place alongside gold-patterned bathroom tiles, and brass door furniture is bound to clash with silvery walls.

**Practicalities** Foil wallcoverings should be hung with special wallpaper paste; ask the supplier for advice. Also take particular care when hanging foil papers around electric sockets and switches since the metal they contain can conduct electricity.

△ **Metallics for warmth**
Chrome and glass furniture can have a rather cold and uninviting feel. This red and silver wallcovering adds warmth to the room and softens the hard outline of the furniture.

◁ **A sumptuous combination**
Glossy black tiles with a diamond design add glamour to any bathroom. Here, they are combined with a few gold-patterned edging tiles, a brass mirror frame and taps to produce a bathroom which is more than a little luxurious.

### △ Mirror magic

*A chimney breast covered in highly reflective mirror tiles undoubtedly focuses attention on the fireplace and adds an enormous amount of light to the room. The shimmering brightness of the tiles is offset by a basically neutral colour scheme of chrome, black, white and grey, with pink accents.*

## MIRROR TILES

Covering alcoves with a mirror or mirror tiles creates an illusion of depth and can help to improve the proportions of a small or narrow room. (Mosaic mirror tiles create a similar effect – but because the mirrored surface is broken up it reflects light and movement, but not true-to-life images.) Install glass shelves and display a collection of objets d'art or glassware to achieve maximum benefit from eye-catching reflections.

### ▷ A hint of glitter

*Plain wall tiles in a bathroom or cloakroom can easily be livened up with a sprinkling of metallic tiles. These two examples illustrate the subtle way in which strips of silver mosaic mirror tiles or narrow golden tiles can add interesting effects to plain white or coloured tiling.*

# DRAMATIC BLACK AND WHITE

## This striking colour combination needs sensitive handling if it is not to become stark and severe.

Disciples of ultra-modern minimalist and high–tech styles of interior decoration adore black and white. It's a colour combination of dramatic simplicity: the ultimate in sophistication. The lines of 'designer' furniture, light fittings and accessories stand out in a room where no other colours distract the eye.

Black and white abounds in nature: dalmations spattered with inky spots, friesian cows and piebald horses are all natural examples of abstract patterns.

The present fashion for black and white started during the 1960s, when the op-art movement inspired a whole era of eye-teasing designs. Today, many of the most up-to-the-minute interiors are based on this combination.

In the 17th and 18th centuries, bedspreads and valances of blackwork embroidery (black thread on white cloth that resembled printed woodcut illustrations) depicting stylized fruit and flowers livened up many an oak four-poster. In both Italian renaissance palaces and the homes of Dutch burghers black and white tiled floors were equally favoured; the Georgians and Victorians, too, used them extensively in kitchens and bathrooms.

So 'no-colour' colour schemes made up largely of black and white needn't be ultra-modern: an eye for the right details in materials and accessories can bring warmth and tradition into this simplest of colour schemes.

△ **Smart and modern**
A black and white scheme highlights detail. The lines of the furniture, the grid of the tiles and even the blinds, provide variety in this room.

▽ **Stark lines**
This simple colour scheme throws into focus the shapes and lines used in a symmetrical arrangement. Any severity is softened by the wood table.

## A GRAPHIC COMBINATION

A colour scheme based on black and white is a courageous choice and needs to be carried out with both consistency and conviction to be effective. Remember that black and white are natural delineators, and so make for a scheme with crisp, clear lines.

Purely black and white living rooms may look wonderfully chic in glossy magazines, but can be difficult to live with on a day-to-day basis. Black and white room schemes are unforgiving of chaos and require tidiness to look good. While too many extra colours can ruin the effect, one accent colour will provide a little visual relief.

The combination of black and white is especially appropriate in kitchens and bathrooms, where these colours enhance an atmosphere of efficiency, order and cleanliness.

Black and white schemes can also be very successful in short-stay rooms such as halls, dining rooms and cloakrooms. Take care, though, to avoid an abrupt colour change from a black and white hall into adjoining rooms; picking out black and white details in a wallpaper border, a rug, or black and white prints and using them in other rooms can lead the eye gently through the transition.

△ *A formal dining room*
*Glossy black furniture combines happily with the fluid lines of a floral paper and more severe striped fabric.*
*See sample board at left.*

▽ *Chequerboard chic*
*A black and white chequerboard floor echoes the rectangular lines of this modern leather and tubular chrome seating.*

## USING BLACK AND WHITE

The use of pattern in black and white schemes demands careful thought: too many severe geometric designs could make the room look more a zebra crossing than anything else. But different black and white patterns can easily be combined; thus floral prints can sit happily with more severe stripes, spots, or checks.

A black and white background makes a natural foil for the clean, sleek lines of modern furniture made of stained wood, plastic, chrome, or leather. As an alternative, try teaming them with the fine details and rich glow of antiques. Black and white ruthlessly draw attention to detail; so whatever furniture you choose, it must be well made and well designed.

Plain white or black floors look stunning, but soon become shabby without meticulous care; ceramic or vinyl tiles, or painted floorboards, make reasonably practical choices for plain floors, while chequerboard patterns add drama. If you prefer carpets, stick to a dark grey or mottled effect rather than plain black or white, which will show every speck of dirt. Avoid creamy carpeting – it will look instantly grubby against true white. A timber floor adds welcome warmth to black and white schemes.

△ **Crisply framed**
Black-painted woodwork crisply frames door-hung storage against a mottled background. Attention to details such as the light switch and door furniture adds the perfect finishing touches.

▽ **A feel for the Thirties**
Lighting is important in black and white rooms. Here, wall-hung fittings provide a warm glow in a potentially severe bathroom. Clever detailing completes the sophisticated theme.

▷ **Pretty nostalgic**
A black and white colour scheme need not appear masculine. A mini-print wallpaper and demurely white bedlinen piled with lacy and frilly cushions soften the austere lines of a black iron bedstead trimmed with brass. The result is a romantic and feminine bedroom.

▽ **City sophistication**
In most black and white kitchens it is the white which predominates; here, though, black flooring and a wall of black tiles are combined with relatively small areas of pure white. However, the room is neither dark nor dreary – white grouting and pale wood-coloured units add lightness and freshness, and the glossy black wall and floor tiles reflect plenty of light.

## RELIEVING THE STARKNESS

Although a colour scheme that's totally black and white can be stunning, the complete absence of anything else makes the eye work overtime searching for hints of colour. So it's usually a good idea to include at least one accent, perhaps on the floor, or in a painting or print. A neutral grey, bright primaries, or rich wood can all relieve the potential starkness of pure black and white. Whatever accent colour you choose, use enough to ensure that its impact isn't swallowed up by the drama of the overall theme.

△ **Fresh green accents**
*Black and white is a very graphic, diagrammatic, combination. Touches of leafy green help to bring these rooms to life.*

△ **A cheerful red** *picture frame, light fitting and tubular furniture brighten up a black and white scheme.*

△ **Primary yellow accents**
*Add zest to white walls and woodwork and a black and white chequerboard floor by using contrasting bright citrus yellow as accent.*

# GRACIOUS GREYS

## Neutral grey doesn't have to be just restrained background to strong colour: it has a character all of its own.

A mix of unadulterated white and black makes grey the purest of neutrals used in decorating. This does not mean, however, that it is simply a flat, dull background colour: far from it. Look at the sky on a stormy day: the variations of shading in the clouds as they move seem infinite.

Grey will pick up and reflect the colours around it, as the clouds reflect tints of pink at sunset. Slate and gunmetal are hard, cold greys that contain an amount of blue – but grey can equally well contain warm hints of yellow or red. Shades of grey can vary from the very pale – almost oyster, it contains so much white – to a graphite so dark it is almost black.

Shiny grey surfaces, particularly silver and stainless steel, reflect the colours around them, adding light and move-ment to a room. As with all textured soft furnishing materials, grey – es-pecially in the darker shades – absorbs light. Grey also has the ability to absorb neighbouring colours, which has the effect of softening the overall look by blurring the edges of other colours as well as the outlines of the room's furniture.

Grey makes an excellent choice for the background to a colour scheme. A graceful dove grey carpet, for example, or grey marble-effect walls, that echo the colours and depth of the real thing, provide a calm and elegant backdrop for vivid furnishings or paintings. Con-versely, grey works equally well as the main colour in a room scheme, es-pecially if it is set off by crisp white paintwork or stylish black lacquered furniture.

△ **Classically elegant**
*Muted blue and mid-grey stripes set the tone for this quietly elegant drawing room, with rust-coloured table lamps providing an accent that emphasizes the rich pine fire surround. The colours are echoed in the woodwork.*

◁ **Modern style**
*Sophisticated grey, white and black are just right for fashionable city living. Here, seating units upholstered in chic silvery grey are clearly outlined against black-varnished wood furniture and pure white walls.*

**MAKING GREY WORK**
Sleek, smooth greys have hidden depths that can be brought out by carefully selecting the accompanying colours. Grey is a simple, easy-to-live-with colour and you might be tempted to overdo its use, but don't let greys completely dominate the room – make them work for you instead. Try combining them with your favourite colours. Whether muted or primary, pale or dark, there's a shade of grey that complements them. A greenish grey, for instance, looks more green when teamed with emerald; a grey with a hint of yellow will take on more of the hue when incorporated into a primrose room scheme.

## TONE AND TEXTURE

It's vital to consider any samples *in situ* since grey has a great propensity to absorb other colours and light. For this reason, tonal balance is particularly important: pale aqua, for instance, can be overwhelmed if it's placed next to a deep charcoal, whereas rich sea-green would balance it perfectly. Similarly, pale pinks or yellows need to be balanced with an equivalent tone of grey, such as dove.

Texture, too, plays an important part with grey, as self-pattern weaves will absorb or reflect light in different quantities, making for interesting variations in shading and tone.

### ▷ *Adding warmth*
*Grey responds well to the natural warmth of wood. Here, the kitchen is saved from appearing clinical by a combination of honey-coloured wood worktops and greenish grey units. The scheme is echoed in the floor treatment.*

### ▽ *Soft greys*
*Greys with a hint of red or yellow can add unexpected warmth. Partnered here by peach curtains that draw out the same colour in the wallpaper, and mushroom shading in the dhurrie, the overall effect is warm and welcoming.*

△ **Spring morning**
Evenly-balanced, hazy stripes of pale peach and silver form the basis for a fresh bedroom look that could brighten the dreariest winter morning. Touches of grey throughout echo the theme.
◁ Fabrics and wallpaper used to make up the scheme.

## ▷ Room for growth

Mid-grey carpet makes a practical choice for a child's room, easily accommodating changing colour schemes. Here a pretty mini-print wallpaper above the dado and discreet blue-grey stripes below are highlighted by the charming border. As the occupant grows up, the basic colours of grey with touches of shining white will form a good background to the brilliant primary colours beloved of small children.

## ▽ Streamlined living

A favourite colour combination is yellow with grey, used in many different shades. This modern dining room has smooth, clean lines that are enhanced by having all the elements in clear dove grey. Equally clear yellow trims on the table, picture frames, skirting board and shelving add colour and serve to frame the whole area.

## ACCENTS TO USE WITH GREY

Grey is ideal to use as background for a room scheme that has to last a long time – you won't tire of it, and almost any colour can be used to jazz it up. Sharp white, in particular, looks crisp and adds clear definition to accent points. In a bathroom, where fixtures and fittings are expensive to replace, grey makes the perfect choice.

△ *Hint of a blush*
*Soft mid-grey tiles and pale blush bath and handbasin are the permanent fixtures. Carpet, blind, paintwork and towel echo these gentle colours.*

▽ *Bright accent colour*
*Grey tiles and carpet, with oyster bath and handbasins, are brightened by touches of orange. Accents like these can be easily switched for a new look.*

# INDEX

PHOTOGRAPHIC CREDITS
Front cover Maison Marie Claire, 1 Bill McLaughlin, 2-3 Dorma, 4-5 Sara
Taylor/Eaglemoss, 6 EWA/Spike Powell, 7 Sara Taylor/Eaglemoss, 8 Arthur Sanderson
and Sons, 9 Sara Taylor/Eaglemoss, 10 EWA/Michael Nicholson, 11(t) Maison Marie
Claire/Duronsay/Pfeufter, 11(b) EWA/Michael Dunne, 12(t) Next Interior,
12(b) Photon/John Hollinshead, 13 Simon Butcher/Eaglemoss, 14(t) Dulux Paints,
14(b) National Magazine Company/David Brittain, 15 Habitat, 16 Perrings, 17(t) Dulux,
17(b) EWA/Jerry Tubby, 18 The Original Bathroom Company, 19 Kuhlman Own Brand
Kitchens, 20-1 National Magazine Company/David Brittain, 21(t) Crown Paints,
21(b) EWA/Spike Powell, 22 & 23(t) EWA/Michael Dunne, 24 & 25 Sara Taylor/
Eaglemoss, 26(t) Dulux, 26(b) Sara Taylor/ Eaglemoss, 27(t) Habitat, 27(b) Curtain Net
Advisory Bureau, 28 Sanderson, 29(t) EWA/Michael Dunne, 29(b) Bill McLaughlin,
30 & 31 Sara Taylor/Eaglemoss, 32(t) EWA, 32(b) Syndication International, 33(t) Dulux
Paints, 33(b) EWA, 34(t) Dulux Paints, 34(b) Camera Press, 35(t) Sue Stowell,
35(b) & 36 Sara Taylor/Eaglemoss, 37 Chris Stephens/Eaglemoss, 38(t) Smallbone of
Devizes, 38(bl) Jalag/Peter Adams, 38-9 & 39(t) Syndication International, 39(b) Crown
Paints, 40 Jerry Tubby/Eaglemoss 41(t) Next Interior, 41(b) PWA International, 42 Mark
Westwood/Eaglemoss, 43 Sara Taylor/Eaglemoss, 44(t) Crown Paints, 44(b) Dulux
Paints, 45(t) EWA/Tom Leighton, 47 Sara Taylor/Eaglemoss, 48 Crown Paints,
48-9 Dulux Paints, 49(t) Next Interior, 49(b) Syndication International, 50(t) Interior
Selection, 50(b) Sara Taylor/Eaglemoss, 51(t) Bill McLaughlin, 51(b) Next Interior,
52 Sara Taylor/Eaglemoss, 53 Hazel Digby/Eaglemoss, 54(t) Maison Marie Claire/
Chabaneix/Peuch, 54(b) Jean-Paul Bonhommet, 55(t) Brian Yates Interiors, 55(b) PWA
International, 56(t) Textra, 56(b) Hazel Digby/Eaglemoss, 57(tl) EWA/Michael Dunne,
57(tr) Smallbone of Devizes, 57(b) PWA International, 58 Hazel Digby/Eaglemoss,
59 Sara Taylor/Eaglemoss, 60(t) Syndication International, 60(b) Houses and Interiors,
61(t) National Magazine Company/David Brittain, 61(b) Bo Appeltoft, 62(t) Pallu and
Lake, 62(b) Arthur Sanderson and Sons, 63 Syndication International, 64 PWA
International, 65 Di Lewis/Eaglemoss, 66 Richard Paul, 67 Jalag, 67(b) EWA/Jerry Tubby,
68 Derwent Upholstery, 69(t) Syndication International, 69(b) National Magazine
Company/John Cook, 71 Di Lewis/Eaglemoss, 72(t) Syndication International,
72(b) Dulux Paints, 73(t) EWA/Jon Bouchier, 73(b) David Hicks International, 74 Next
Interior, 75(t) National Magazine Company/Peter Anderson, 75(b) EWA/Michael Dunne,
76(t) Schreiber Furniture Ltd, 76(b) Sara Taylor/Eaglemoss, 77 Di Lewis/Eaglemoss,
78(t) Richard Paul, 78(b) David Hicks, 79 Textra, 80(t) EWA/Clive Helm, 80(b) EWA/
Michael Crockett, 81(t) EWA/Neil Lorimer, 81(b) Capital Tile Supplies, 82 EWA/Michael
Crockett, 83 Di Lewis/Eaglemoss, 84(t) Ken Kirkwood, 84(b) Richard Paul, 85(t) Arthur
Sanderson and Sons, 85(br) Syndication International, 86 PWA International,
87(t) Syndication International, 87(b) Hygena, 89 Sara Taylor/Eaglemoss,
90(t) Syndication International, 90(b) EWA/Michael Dunne, 91(t) Zanussi, 91(b) National
Magazine Company/David Brittain, 92 Smallbone of Devizes, 93(t) Syndication
International, 93(b) National Magazine Company/David Brittain, 94 Armitage Shanks